The Terebinth Journal

A Biblically Based Life Recovery Workbook

Kathleen Olmert and Cynthia Catlett

FIRST EDITION

ISBN: 978-1-953576-44-6

Published by

Certa PUBLISHING

3741 Linden Avenue SE | Grand Rapids, MI 49548

Printed in the United States

"Then Abram moved his tent,

and went and dwelt by the

TEREBINTH trees of Mamre,

which are in Hebron,

and built an altar there to the Lord."

Genesis 13:18 (NKJV)

Introduction

Getting from point A to point Z in the journey of life can often be a huge struggle. We can follow steps and guidelines to help us get to where we want to be, but many times the goal seems just out of reach.

What if we start by asking ourselves some really tough questions. Questions that come straight from the Word of God, which is always our guideline for healing and renewal. These are questions that, Biblically speaking, go back to the beginning of time. Ageless questions, haunting questions, and healing questions that God Himself asks His people.

This journal is designed to be used as a tool for individuals or small groups who desire healing, restoration, peace and a life filled with hope. Take the next thirty days and journal your way through these questions. Some may be easy for you to answer, some may be really tough. But stick with the questions. Dig deep into the Word of God, read, study and do the work. Dig deep into yourself. You will be amazed at what you find.

Nothing worthwhile comes without effort.

Day 1

Question: Did God really say that?

Genesis 3:1 "Now the serpent was more crafty than any of the wild animals the Lord God had made. He said to the woman, Did God really say, You must not eat of the fruit from any tree in the garden?"

The very first question we see in God's Word brings up the issue of doubt:

Doubt in the very existence and reality of God

Doubt in the reality of the truth of what God speaks

Doubt in the belief that God loves his children, his family

This first question – the question of all questions – is introduced to mankind by the enemy of his soul, the enemy of God Himself, Satan. All that has to happen for any one of us to make a wrong move, or take a wrong turn in life, or make a wrong choice, is for the voice of doubt to seep into our thought process.

God's response in Genesis 3:11 shows us His heart toward us, and how He feels about His children. He says to Eve, "What have you done?" I imagine this as a question of great sorrow and grief, for God's desire for His children was that they live a life filled with grace and freedom. And so, His heart cries out to them asking, what have you done?

Doubt is like poisonous sarin gas, all it has to do is seep into the cracks and into the air around us to start the dying process. If the poisonous gas is not shut off, we will die.

It is the same thing that happens when doubt starts to seep into our thinking process. The end result is spiritual death.

It is interesting to see in the Scriptures that the very first question asked is the one pertaining to doubt. There must be a reason.

Doubt is toxic, so it must be addressed first in our lives.

Look at how the enemy works. Up until this point in creation, mankind was pure of heart and mind and thought, the way God created them to be. The moment the enemy was able to introduce doubt into the thinking process of man, the dying process began.

The death process could have been stopped, or canceled by a single word: NO! But it wasn't.

The "doubt" possibility was introduced to mankind right here, at this point. Eve didn't say no. Adam didn't say no. And the lives of all mankind were changed forever.

Where did doubt first enter your life? How did it come? Did you doubt that God is real and alive and active in your world because there is too much death and destruction everywhere?

Did doubt come because you didn't feel loved? And if you weren't loved, then how can there be a God who loves?

Did doubt come because someone else introduced a toxic "thought" into your life? Someone let loose a small whiff of deadly "sarin gas" into your thought process? Someone introduced you to a doubt so huge that it killed any sense of hope and truth?

What doubts do you struggle with today? List them all and give them to the One who can cancel all doubt, even if you are struggling to believe that.

____

____

____

____

____

You can get past the doubt in your life. It is a process. It will take time. It will take honesty. It will require you to be real about the person you have been up to this point in your life.

Prayer for Day 1:

Heavenly Father, Almighty God, my God and my creator, I want to believe that what You say is true. I want to believe that You are real, that You can do what You say You can do, but I have all of these doubts filling my mind and it is really hard for me to believe right now. I want this to change, I want to believe in You and all that You are, so today, right now, I give all of this doubt to You, trusting that You will help move me from doubt to truth. In Jesus' Name, Amen.

Scripture Reading for Day 1:

Genesis 2:1 through 3:7

Day 1 Life Challenge Questions:

What have you believed about God your whole life?

What do you believe about God today?

Day 2

Question: Where are you?

Genesis 3:9 "But the Lord God called to the man, where are you?"

Where are you? The second question in Scripture. This comes right after the seed of doubt was sown into mankind's thinking.

God knows that doubt has entered the hearts and minds of His children. He knows that doubt has caused confusion and shame in their lives. And He knows that they are hiding from Him, avoiding Him. And in His love, He calls out to them and asks, where are you? Where are you, why are you hiding from me? Have you done what I did not want you to do and allowed doubt to enter your mind? Where are you? I am looking for you, why are you hiding from me?

God's question to each one of us is always, where are you? Right now, right here, where are you?

God longs to love you, but you have to come out of hiding in order to allow His love to fill you. You have to stop avoiding Him in order for His love to fill you.

You may have become very good at hiding, at blending into the world around you, yet God still calls you to step out and allow yourself to be found by Him. He calls you to come out of hiding and allow yourself to be loved. He says to you today:

No more hiding in doubt

No more hiding in fear

No more hiding in anger

No more hiding in self-hatred

No more hiding in insecurity

No more hiding in darkness

Hiding can feel safe. Hiding creates a space for you to be alone. Hiding creates distance from others. Hiding creates distance from God. Hiding keeps everyone and everything at arm's length from you.

He says to you today, I am looking for you but you are running away from me. I want you to return to me so that I can pour my love into you.

No more hiding. No more distance. No more avoiding.

God says to you today, it is time to come out of hiding, take one step and move toward the Light of My love today.

What has hiding looked like in your past?

In what ways are you hiding from God today?

Prayer for Day 2:

Dear Heavenly Father, I realize that I have been hiding for a long, long time. I have no idea how to even come out of this hiding place I am in, so I ask for Your help today. I need Your help to show me the way to walk. Shine Your light into the darkness of my hiding today, and show me the way out. Help me to take Your hand and take one step at a time into the warmth of Your light and love. Shine Your love light into my darkest places today. In Jesus' Name, Amen.

Scripture Reading for Day 2:

Genesis 3: 8 – 24

Day 2 Life Challenge Questions:

What beliefs are keeping you hidden from God?

How have these beliefs affected your life decisions up to this point?

Day 3

Question: Who told you that you were naked?

Genesis 3:10-11 "He answered, I heard you in the garden, and I was afraid because I was naked, so I hid. And He (God) said, who told you that you were naked?"

The third question in Scripture we find God asking man, who told you this? In other words, who said this to you? Whose voice are you listening to?

Voices come at us from every direction right from the moment we are born. Good voices, bad voices, indifferent voices.

When we are children, the voices around us have a tendency to mold us and shape us into who we become as adults. When we are young, tender and vulnerable, we believe the voices we hear, whether good or bad. Sometimes it's one voice over and over that shapes us – sometimes its many voices over a long period of time that shape us.

The question we need to ask ourselves today is; were the voices we heard actually carrying the truth of who we are? Or has it been a lie the whole time? Are those voices and the things they said still true of us today?

What did the voice of "doubt" say to you?

What did the voice of "not good enough" say to you?

What did the voice of "not worthy of love" say to you?

What did the voice of "not smart enough" say to you?

Maybe it's time to start listening to a different voice, the voice of the One who created you and knows you from the inside out. The One who is asking you now; "who told you that?" Your Heavenly Father says to you today, it was not Me.

Today, He asks you to hear a new voice, His voice, the true voice that speaks over you and into you and through you. The voice that says to you, *you are mine.* I made you and I have plans for you that you don't even know about yet, plans that will be wonderful for you. His voice says to you, *I have chosen you, and I love you, and you are mine.*

Part of the process of learning how to hear truth from God begins by learning how to study the Bible. This is where you will find truth. You must look at what God's word says about You. God's written word is here to teach you and lead you. Start small, look up a few of these verses and read them for yourself. Write down the verses that speak to you and strengthen you. Begin to memorize them; tape them to your bathroom mirror, your refrigerator, your desk. Let the truth of God's Word mold you into who you really are.

Make a list of some of the lies that you have believed in the past:

____

____

____

____

____

Do any of these lies still feel true today?

____

____

____

Can you begin the process of believing the truth about who God says you are?

____

____

____

Prayer for Day 3:

Dear Father, I have listened to the wrong voices all of my life, but no more. Today I take a stand and I say no more. The voices are just that, old. I choose to shut out the old and replace them with new. I am learning a new way to live and I am asking for Your help as I learn how to do this. Let Your voice ring loud, true and strong within me today and every day! In Jesus' Name, Amen.

Scripture Reading for Day 3:

(The general meaning of each verse is paraphrased next to the verse reference.
Take the time to look each one up and write them out in full.)

Romans 8:1-2 – I am free from condemnation
Romans 8:28 – I am assured that all things work together for good in my life
Romans 8:35-39 – I cannot be separated from the love of God
Philippians 3:20 – I am a citizen of heaven
Philippians 1:6 – I am confident that the good work
that God began in me will be perfected
2 Corinthians 1:21-22 – I have been established, anointed and sealed by God
John 15:16 – I have been chosen and appointed
to bear fruit (produce good things)
2 Timothy 1:7 – I have not been given a spirit of fear,
but of power, love and a sound mind
Hebrews 4:16 – I find grace and mercy in time of need
Philippians 4:13 – I can do all things through Christ who gives me strength
Ephesians 1:5 – I have been adopted as God's child

Day 3 Life Challenge Questions:

What is the loudest voice in your life right now?

What is that voice telling you about you?

Is that voice bringing you life or is it bringing you death?

Day 4

Question: What have you done?

Genesis 3:13 "Then the Lord God said to the woman, what is this you have done?"

For most of us, the question of what we have done is a huge question, and for many of us, the answers are really hard.

Looking back into what we have done hurts, but know this, there is hope. How?

The things we have done were the result of many things – the choices we made, the choices others made for us, the circumstances we found ourselves in at the time, our surroundings, our culture, our family… the list goes on. All of these things play a part in what we have done.

But, what we have done does not define who we are. We all make mistakes. Big ones, small ones, terrible ones.

What we have done is **NOT** who we are! What we have done is **NOT** who we are!

Let that sink in. Your past does not define you. You can't change the things that have already happened, you can only change what you will do in the future: today, tomorrow, and forever.

What you have done will define you if you do not give it to God. Pick up your past, hold it in your hands and lay it on the ground before God.

He already knows all you have done. You have to be the one to give it up to Him. He will not take it from you if you do not offer it up to Him.

We were not created or designed to carry the weight and the burden of our past. We must hand it to God. We ask for forgiveness. Forgiveness for ourselves. Forgiveness for others. Forgiveness from others. Give it all to God, He can handle it, we can't.

How can you take the "what have I done" accusations in your life and give it to God today? Once and for all.

____

____

Do you believe He can carry the burden of your past?

____

____

Do you want to be relieved of that burden?

____

____

What do you have to do right now to be relieved of that burden?

____

____

When you give those "what have I done" accusations to the Lord, and ask for His help and His forgiveness, the Bible tells us that He forgives and then He forgets. He says it is forgotten as far as the east is from the west.

So, do it! Give it to Him, and let it go!

Because our minds are programmed to remember, memories come back. We are told in 2 Corinthians 10:5 to "take every thought captive" which means that we are to grab that thought, that memory, and take it captive and say "no," not today. This is forgiven and it is under the blood of Jesus and I leave it there.

This takes time to master. You may have to say "no" and take those thoughts captive one hundred times a day, until your mind remembers the new truth: "*it is not who I am!*"

Prayer for Day 4:

Oh Lord God, the things I have done! You know each and every one of them, and you know the circumstances surrounding each and every one of them. You knew me then, and You know me now. Help me today to remember that my past does not define me. My past is not me. I hold on to a new and beautiful future that You, Father, are laying out before me and helping me to walk in. So, today, I give all of my past to You. Take it Lord, I don't want to carry it anymore! In Jesus' Name, Amen.

Scripture Reading for Day 4:

2 Corinthians 10:1-5

Day 4 Life Challenge Question:

God doesn't look at what you have done.
He looks at who you are.

Who does God say that you are?

Luke 1:68 ____

2 Corinthians 5:17______________________________________

Romans 8:16 ____

Galatians 5:1 ____

Psalm 139:14____

Romans 8:37 ____

John 6:63____

Day 5

Question: Why are you angry?

Genesis 4:6 "Then the Lord said to Cain, why are you angry? Why is your face downcast?"

As the saying goes: what goes into a man, comes out of a man. The same is true for our emotions. Anger, which is the second emotion, shows up on our faces and in our actions. It can lay dormant inside of us for years. Whether it is buried deep inside of us, or always spewing out from us, *it always shows up on our face first.*

Sadness, fear, anger. Emotions that spring forth from the inner depths of our being, many times without so much as a warning.

We think we are pretty good at hiding it, but God, our Heavenly Father knows all about it. He knows all of it. So He asks us, "Why are you angry? Why are you sad?"

Our response is usually something like this: "you just don't understand, no one understands."

That is just not true. God sees. God knows. God understands.

The next response we usually have is: then why? How could God see and know and not stop it all from happening?

We need to ask some questions that may help us to understand.

Does every man and every woman have free will and are they allowed to make their own choices? (Yes)

What do you think, or what have you always believed?______________________

____

If God knows everything, then isn't He capable of stopping the wrong choices or the bad choices that people make? Yes, but He doesn't because if He reached down and manipulated every life choice, every circumstance, every situation, then we humans are not free agents, but robots living life at the hand of a controller.

God's design for us from the time that mankind was placed on earth, was for us to walk in harmony, fellowship and friendship with Him, and with each other.

Giving mankind the option of free will allows each of us to make choices every day, all day, all of our lives. The earth is filled with millions of people who constantly make choices that are good, or evil or right or wrong. These choices don't only affect them, they affect the lives of other people around them. This happens in nations, in cities, in towns, in neighborhoods and in families.

Good choices affect others. Bad choices affect others, sometimes in horrific ways.

We, God's children, are called to step out of making wrong choices and step into fellowship and friendship with Him. As we do this, we begin to learn how to make our choices based upon His Word, and His goodness.

God's greatest desire is for each of us to walk beside Him, to learn of Him and to become like Him. But it is a choice. We get to choose. God will not force us. He calls to us. So our choice today must be to answer that call and step out into a journey of truly discovering who God is. Choosing to take this step moves us toward making better choices, and ultimately to making good choices.

Choosing to take this step and beginning the journey of relationship with God starts dissolving roots of anger and bitterness.

Choosing to understand the nature of God and His all-consuming love for us, starts dissolving roots of distrust and fear.

Know what is true – God does see all and knows all. He sees your pain, your anger, your questions. He cannot force others to make the right decisions, just as He could not force those who hurt you, to not hurt you. They will suffer the consequences of their own choices. You are here right now because you have been called out to be set free from what has held you captive, whether it is fear, anger or distrust.

God, your Father says to you today: "Trust Me. Walk with Me and learn all about Me so that I can help you release the roots of pain, anger and fear. Choose Me today."

How can you begin to release some of your deep-seated emotions to God today?

Does that seem impossible to you? Why?

Can you wrap your mind around the thought that God loves you enough to give you the right to choose between right or wrong, good or bad?

If you have made poor choices in the past, are you ready to begin making good choices for yourself today? What could be your first step?

Prayer for Day 5:

Father, this is so hard for me. Everything that is inside of me screams and hates the wrong things that were done to me, and the wrong things I have done. The choices made weren't always mine to make and that too makes me angry. Help me Father, today, to step out and make the choice to walk beside You and to learn all that I can about You and Your ways. Thank you for opening my mind and my ears to be able to grasp and understand You. Take my hand and help me walk beside You, one step at a time. In Jesus' Name, Amen.

Scripture Reading for Day 5:

Genesis 4:1-7
Galatians 5: 22-23

Day 5 Life Challenge Question:

If anger is the second emotion, then hurt is the first emotion. Can you go back and find the hurt that has produced anger or maybe even a deep-seated rage within you? It could be more than one incident. Write it down. Take it to Jesus. Be honest with Him about the emotions you felt at the time.

Day 6

Question: Where is your brother?

Genesis 4:9 "Then the Lord said to Cain, where is your brother Abel? I don't know, he replied. Am I my brother's keeper?"

There is concern in this question. God is asking Cain where his brother is. God knows that Abel is sitting right next to Him in the heavenly realm because Cain has murdered him and released him from the earth.

This is the first recorded act of death after the choice Adam and Eve made to disobey God. It doesn't take mankind long to walk in the way of evil once that decision had been made.

Cain thinks that he is fine, he thinks no one knows what he has done, but God sees and God knows and God calls him out on it. "Where is your brother?"

Cain's response to God was rather curt and sharp, "Am I my brother's keeper?" In other words, how should I know and why should I care?

What was buried in Cain's heart showed up on his face. God knows.

Cain's curt comment showed unconcern. God calling him out on it was God's way of saying, "but you are supposed to be concerned." We all are.

Our tendency is to watch our own backs, take care of ourselves first, look out for number one. This is what our culture teaches us, but it is not what God teaches us. God's design and desire for us is to live in fellowship and friendship with each other. God's desire is for us to walk in harmony with Him and with our fellow man.

We were designed to care for each other and to love each other. We *are* our brother's keepers. We *are* supposed to care, nurture and love those around us. It is part of God's plan for us.

We will never be able to love ourselves as we should until we are able to love others. And, just as true, we can never truly love others, until we love ourselves.

As God's children we are called to love, because He is love. We are not called to judge, we are called to love. That can be a really hard thing for us to do. How do we love people who are mean and evil? How do we love people who hurt other people?

We have to begin to think the way God thinks. God loves people, all people, yet at times, He hates what they do. We are called to love all people, but we don't have to like what they do. We are called to show love, not unconcern. We are called to take care of one another, not to harm one another.

If we can't personally get out there and help others, then we need to bless and support those who do. Start showing love today. Start being concerned about others today.

How easy is it for you to like or love other people, especially people who are not like you?

____

____

How easy is it for you to like or love people who have hurt you?

____

____

____

Are you able to reach out and help others who are in need, or is this hard for you to do? If so, what do you think makes it so hard?

____

____

____

____

Prayer for Day 6:

Father, today, I ask for You to help me learn how to love like You love. Help me to look past people's faults and see them as You see them, its certainly different than how I see them. Let my eyes and my heart be filled with love for others. Let the words that come out of my mouth be full of love for others. In Jesus' Name, Amen.

Scripture Reading for Day 6:

James 1:27
Proverbs 17:17
Matthew 5:38-40

Day 6 Life Challenge Questions:

We will never be able to love ourselves as we should until we are able to love others. And, just as true, we can never truly love others, until we love ourselves.

Where is your heart with loving you? Do you love yourself?

Do you know that you are loved by the God of the Universe? It is this love that will enable you to love others.

Do you know, really know, that you are loved by God? How do you know this? Be honest with yourself and with God.

Day 7

Question: Oh, Sovereign Lord, what can you give me?

Genesis 15:2-3 "But Abram said, oh, Sovereign Lord, what can you give me since I remain childless and the one who will inherit my estate is Eliezer of Damascus? And Abram said, You have given me no children, so a servant in my household will be my heir."

Abraham learned to walk with God and to hear His voice. God spoke to him and asked him to leave his home and his family and to step out into a journey with Him.

God asked Abraham to trust Him, and to follow Him, and he did.

Abraham spent many years learning all about God and His ways. He chose to find out all that he could about this God who had picked him out of a crowd and called to him.

As he walked with God on a daily basis, he began to learn how to trust Him. God tells Abraham that if he will follow Him and if he will trust Him, that He will bless him, his children, grandchildren and their children. God says that a multitude of generations would be blessed because of the choice that Abraham would make.

Abraham reaches a fork in the road of his life at this point. He had a choice to make. He could follow and believe this God he was learning from, or he could pack up and go back home to his family and the ways of life he once knew.

But Abraham asks God a question. How can this happen since I am old and I don't have any children?

God answers and says, make the choice to walk with Me and trust Me and I will bless you and all of your family.

God doesn't answer Abraham with the how He will do it, He answers with the why. God says to him, I know it sounds impossible, but trust Me and watch what I can do.

Abraham did choose to trust, and yes, he was blessed with a huge family, too many to number!

Can you trust God today to take the nothing that you have and allow Him to turn it into something?

Do you know that God has picked you out of the crowd – and needs you to do something for Him?

Prayer for Day 7

Father, today I give You my nothing, for I have nothing, and I ask You to bless this nothing and turn it into something. Help me to believe that if You can do it for Abraham, as Your Word says, then You can do it for me. Help me to trust completely in You today. In Jesus' Name, Amen.

Scripture Reading for Day 7:

Genesis Chapter 15
Luke 1:26-38

Day 7 Life Challenge Questions:

Abraham learned to walk with God. He was obedient. It was not an instant thing. Are you willing to learn what walking with God looks like?

Are you at a point in your life that you want to walk with God more than you want anything else in life?

How desperate are you to have God in your life?

Why are you desperate for God in your life?

Day 8

Question: Where have you come from and where are you going?

Genesis 16:8 "And he said, Hagar, slave of Sarai, where have you come from, and where are you going? I am running away from my mistress Sarai, she answered."

We all tend to want to take the easy way out, just like Hagar. Just run away. Avoid. Dismiss. Deny.

Hagar too, was running. Hagar was tired of being treated badly and she was tired of crying. And so she ran.

Running shoves us out into the wastelands, out into the desert, the wilderness. It's scary and dry and dark. Hagar fell down weeping and crying and suddenly an angel of God calls her by name and asks her a question. Where did you come from, and more importantly, where are you going?

Finding ourselves in the wilderness of despair, depression, fear, or loneliness should cause us to stop and ask the same question.

Where did we come from? What's behind us?

Where are we going? What's ahead of us?

Are we leaving behind the ugly, the bad, the barren and moving forward to the new and the possible?

—or—

Are we looking behind us at what was there and thinking it will never change?

Are we looking at what was hard and broken and painful and thinking that it is better than the unknown that lies ahead?

Take a moment and look back to where you came from – do you want to go back?

You can, the choice is yours to make.

Now take a moment and look forward to what could be, to what is possible – it may look scary, but you are learning to walk a new way and a new path, with God at your side – and with God beside you, the possibilities are endless.

Go backward, or go forward?

Where have you come from? Where are you going?

You may not be able to answer this question right now but keep thinking about it. Don't let it go!

Where have I come from?

Where am I going?

Prayer for Day 8

Father, my heart says I really don't want to go back where I was – but my mind says it would be easier. I have listened to my mind for far too long and it is time for me to start listening to my heart. Help me today, Father, to be true to what You are telling me, deep in my heart, help me today to see and envision all the possibilities that lie before me. In Jesus' Name, Amen.

Scripture Reading for Day 8:

Jeremiah 29:11

Day 8 Life Challenge Questions:

Do you believe that you have a future worth living for?

What does that future look like in your mind?

How does God have your future? Does He have it?

Do you know that there is so much more to this life than what you have experienced? How are you made for more in this life?

Day 9

Question: Who are you?

Genesis 27:32 "His father Isaac asked him, Who are you?"

There was some confusion and deception going on here in this part of Genesis. Isaac is very old, on his death bed, almost blind and probably a little hard of hearing. He knew it was time to pronounce the family blessing on the oldest male child, which was Esau.

Esau goes out to the field to find food to bring to his father for the ceremonial blessing and while he is gone, Jacob, Esau's brother, sneaks into Isaac's tent and pretends to be Esau. Isaac's eyes are dim, yet he detects something a bit off so he asks, who are you?

A family blessing was at stake, a family history was being set up and an identity had to be made. Who are you?

A great question for us today. Who are we, really?

There may have been some confusion and some deception in and around our past, possibly even brought on by those in our family who were supposed to love us and cherish us. Our identity was stolen. It is time to take it back.

Who are you?

We have to take that question to the only one who can answer it. God, our Father, our Creator. He is the one who gives us our identity. He is the truthful one that tells us who we really are.

He alone has the authority to show us our true identity because He is the one who made us. He is the one who made us in His image, in His likeness.

We may have this particular last name, or come from that particular blood line, but it is our spiritual identity and our spiritual bloodline – through Jesus Christ – that tells us who we really are.

Being born into the Kingdom of God, through faith in Jesus, transfers us into heirs, sons, daughters, children of Almighty God. We become His and only His.

How do we know this? He tells us so in His Word.

Romans 8:14: "For those who are led by the Spirit of God are the children of God."

Romans 8:17: "Now, if we are children, then we are heirs – heirs of God and co-heirs with Christ…"

Galatians 4:7: "So, you are no longer a slave, but God's child; and since you are his child, God has made you also an heir."

2 Corinthians 6:18 "I will be a Father to you, and you will be my sons and daughters, says the Lord Almighty."

Ask yourself today: Who am I?

Who does your mind tell you that you are?

____

____

____

Who does your heart (emotions) tell you that you are?

____

____

____

Who does God say that you are?

____

____

____

Prayer for Day 9

Prayer: Father, today, my heart and mind long to believe that what You say about me is true. This is hard for me to grasp. Please help me today to understand my new identity in You. Help me to understand what that actually means. And help me right now, from this point forward, to walk faithfully and strongly in this new identity that You have given to me. In Jesus' Name, Amen.

Scripture Reading for Day 9:

2 Corinthians 5:17
1 Corinthians 2:7–16

Day 9 Life Challenge Questions:

Who do others say you are?

How has your past defined you? Can you let this past go?

What is the truth about who you are according to God's Word?

Day 10

Question: What is your name?

Genesis 32:27 "The man asked him, what is your name? Jacob, he answered."

Names. The Bible is filled with names. Our lives are filled with names. People we know, people we don't know but know of, famous people, average people, poor people, rich people... on and on the list could go.

Someone mentions a name and we immediately have a mental picture of that person.

Names are attached to mental images. Our name is attached to a mental image in someone else's mind.

Ask yourself, is the mental image that someone else has of me really me? Is that who I really am? Were my actions at one time in my life brought on by my circumstances, or by my own choices at that time? Is that really who I am? Is it who I want to be from now on?

Hard questions. Hard questions that must be answered to be able to move forward.

We cannot change what has happened in the past, we can only work on today which will produce good or bad results for us tomorrow.

Admitting the mistakes of our past helps us push past them. If who we once were is not who we want to be, then a new choice has to be made.

I *choose* to be different today, right now.

In the scripture referenced above, Jacob, the deceiver, had to leave his home and family because of his trickery. He fled to another part of the country and lived with his Uncle Laban for twenty years.

You can grow up and mature a lot in twenty years, and Jacob had. It was time for him to return to his homeland and his family, but he was afraid that his brother Esau would still hate him because of what he had done. God tells Jacob to go back home, so he does.

One night as he is journeying home, he has a very vivid and spiritual encounter with an angel of the Lord. The angel asks him what his name is and he answers and says "Jacob," which in Hebrew means deceiver. The angel says to him, "your name will no longer be Jacob, but Israel, because you have struggled with God, and with men, and have overcome."

Something had happened to Jacob in those twenty years away from home. He grew up. He matured. No longer was he a manipulator and deceiver. God Himself calls him by a new name, Israel, meaning, God preserves and keeps. Jacob's destiny was not tied to his old name, it was attached to his new name.

Today make the choice to call yourself by a new name. The old name that others called you, or that you called yourself, is no longer who you are.

No longer is your name stupid…

No longer is your name worthless…

No longer is your name ugly…

No longer is your name thief…

No longer is your name lazy…

No longer is your name addict…

No longer is your name unfit…

No longer is your name lacking…

No longer is your name anger…

No longer is your name fearful…

Whatever name you have been called in the past is not who you are.

Those who receive Jesus Christ as their Lord and Savior receive a new name, it goes along with your new identity in Christ.

I am chosen	*I am forgiven*	*I am called*
I am brand new	*I am strong*	*I am courageous*

What name or names were you once known by:

____

____

Is that who you really are today?

____

Are you ready to receive a new name today?

____

____

Prayer for Day 10:

Prayer: Father in Heaven, I do not want to be remembered or known by what I use to be. I do not want to be known by my old names. Help me today to choose to walk in the strength and power of Jesus Christ and in the new name that He has for me. In Jesus' Name, Amen.

Scripture Reading for Day 10:

Genesis Chapter 32
Genesis 17: 3-7
Revelation 2:17

Day 10 Life Challenge Questions:

Can you sit with this thought for a moment? Jesus wants to give you a new name and a new identity. STOP! Listen! In this quiet, what new name are you hearing? Ask Him for a new name. Remember, He wants to give you a new name and a new identity because His desire is for you.

LET HIM!!!

Day 11

Question: What are you looking for?

Genesis 37:14-15 "So he said to him, Go and see if all is well with your brothers and with the flocks, and bring word back to me. Then he sent him off from the valley of Hebron. When Joseph arrived in Shechem, a man found him wandering around in the fields and asked him, what are you looking for?"

Aren't we always looking for something? We humans seem to need something different all the time. Something to make things better, or sometimes we just need something to change in our circumstances. It seems we are never quite satisfied with where we are or what we have, we are always looking – and usually in the wrong places.

In the scripture reference above, we see Joseph, the favored son, the good son, the dreaming son, being sent off to a distant place to find his older brothers. The brothers have taken their herd of sheep to greener pastures and they have been away from home for a long time. Their father Jacob (Israel) wants to know how his boys are doing so he sends Joseph on a journey.

Joseph is wandering around in the area he believes his brothers to be in but can't find them. Someone stops him and asks him what he is looking for. "My brothers, have you seen them?" he says. The man points him in the right direction.

Joseph believes his brothers will be happy to see him, but the brothers are much older and they despise Joseph because of the dreams he has had in the past. When they finally meet up, the brothers plot to destroy him. They grab him and sell him to traders who take him away to Egypt as a slave.

Imagine Joseph's surprise at being grabbed, tied, sold – by those that were supposed to love him. What must have been going through Joseph's heart and mind as this was happening to him? Anger? Fear? Betrayal of the worst kind?

What should have been an "average" scheduled trip to find his brothers, turns into a journey of danger, fear and injustice.

But God...

Why? *He was needed*. Joseph was needed in God's Kingdom for God's plans.

Joseph perseveres and gets through the hard times and the tough times. He survives it all. And suddenly he moves from captivity to freedom – then from freedom to leadership – from leadership to ruling and reigning at the top of the kingdom with the king.

One of the greatest scriptures is found here near the end of Joseph's story when years later he is reunited with his brothers. They are so afraid that Joseph, now a man of great power, will have them killed for what they did to him as a child. But Joseph tells them not to worry because *what they had intended as harm, God used as good to help them all.* (Gen 50:19-20)

We too, are to be used of God for something good. Do you believe that? Do you believe that your search for "something" can be turned into "something" good – for the benefit of others? Look up and read Jeremiah 29:11

In all of your searching for something, God has been searching for you!

Is it hard for you to believe that God has been searching for you? Why?

____

____

Is it hard for you to believe that God has plans for your life? Why?

____

____

Is it hard for you to believe that God, the one who created you, can take your mess and turn it into something beautiful? Because He can.

Do you believe that your story can be used to help others? How?

____

____

Do you believe that what was meant to harm you or destroy you, can now be used to pull others out of harmful situations and paths of destruction?

What is it that you continue to look for?

Prayer for Day 11:

Prayer: Father, I just have to say it here, and now… I hate what my life was. I hate everything about it. I hate everything that tried to destroy me and I give that hate to you. Father, I ask You to help me move away from hate and into purpose. Help me to lay hate at your feet and help me to pick up love, kindness and forgiveness in its place. Help me to understand that You are what I have always been searching for. Show me how You, Father, can take my past and use it for Your good, and for the good of others. In Jesus' Name, Amen.

Scripture Reading for Day 11:

Jeremiah 29:11
Genesis 37: 12-36
Genesis 45: 1-15
Genesis 50:15-21

Day 11 Life Challenge Questions:

How do you feel you are needed for the Kingdom?

Has God given you a dream that seems impossible? What is that dream? (Remember God has no limits!)

Day 12

Question: What shall I tell them?

Exodus 3:13 "Moses said to God, suppose I go to the Israelites and say to them, the God of your fathers has sent me to you, and they ask me, what is his name, then what shall I tell them?"

Moses, another servant and child of God, like Joseph before him, and Jesus after him, had attempts on his life from the day of his birth.

Moses is moved from his family of slaves where there was danger and peril, into the protection and safety of the Egyptian palace. There he grows and matures in wisdom and knowledge, just as Joseph had. Moses is Jewish, not Egyptian, and he knows it, and he sees many things in the Egyptian kingdom that bother him.

One day in a fit of rage and anger he kills an Egyptian and has to run for his life. He runs until he finds himself in the wilderness and there he hides. He hides for forty years and during those years, life goes on, and he marries and becomes a shepherd, a tender of sheep. A far cry from the palace and its privileges.

But it is there in the desert, in the smell of sheep and hot sand, in the unfamiliar, in the new way of life, that God finds him. God makes himself known to him in a very real and tangible way. A bush is on fire, but not consumed, and in the awe of that moment, God speaks to Moses. He speaks to him and calls him and draws Moses to him - *because he is needed.* God tells Moses to go back to Egypt and tell the king to set the slaves, the children of Israel, free.

Moses has some doubts about this assignment for sure. He questions God and asks why the Israelites would believe him. Then he says, "and if they ask who you are, what do I tell them?"

"God said to Moses, I AM WHO I AM. This is what you are to say to the Israelites: I AM has sent me to you." (Exodus 3:14)

"I AM." That is a strange way to answer Moses. What God is saying is:

I AM able to deliver you

I AM able to free you

I AM able to help you

I AM able to set the captives free

I AM able to renew

I AM able to restore

I AM able to work everything out for your good

I AM able to change your future

I AM able to change your story

I AM able to make all things new

I AM able to forgive

I AM able to do whatever you need me to do

In other words, God declares that He is able to be what you need Him to be at any time, anywhere.

We don't all get the burning bush experience to find God, He reaches out to each of us in a way that we will accept and understand. Whatever our experience is like, we do get to choose. Do we hear, do we try to understand, do we search for answers, do we press in and long for more of God? Or do we turn away and turn back to the menial day to day lives we once had.

If Moses had turned his back on the burning bush, the thing he could not comprehend or understand, then he would have turned his back on hearing the voice of God, he would have turned his back on his destiny, and he would have turned his back on the millions of people he could help.

How have you experienced the presence of God in your life so far?

If you are struggling with this concept, what is it you desire to know?

Look up and read Philippians 4:6, what does this verse tell you to do?

Prayer for Day 12:

Prayer: Heavenly Father, the Great I AM, I come before You today asking that You would make Yourself known to me in a greater way. Help me to learn to study Your Word and dig deep into the knowledge of You. If there is a divine purpose and destiny for me, I ask that You would help me understand this and move and live the way You would want me to live. I trust that when I am ready, You will make your plans clear to me. In Jesus' Name, Amen.

Scripture Reading for Day 12:

Exodus 2:11 – 3:15

Day 12 Life Challenge Questions:

God says that you are needed. Where are you needed?

Who depends on you and needs you?

How has God been there for you?

What happened in your past that has made you feel like you are not needed or wanted?

Now take this to the Father in prayer. Write out your prayer to your loving Father:

Day 13

Question: Who will be going?

Exodus 10:8 "Then Moses and Aaron were brought back to Pharaoh, Go worship the Lord your God, he said. But tell me who will be going?"

Moses is obedient to God, returns to Egypt and approaches the king, the Pharaoh, to ask him to release the Jewish people – to set them free, to release them from captivity.

Pharaoh doesn't want to set the people free, he owns them, uses them, abuses them. And he needs them for the continued growth of his kingdom. The pharaoh's life is a life of staggering wealth because of the "free" labor of the people he has enslaved.

God steps in and says, "enough." He sends Moses, his servant, a leader, a shepherd, a protector, to step in and ask for the life and freedom of His people.

Days, weeks, months go by and Moses keeps asking, and Pharaoh keeps saying no. After a barrage of plagues and calamities brought on by Pharaoh's refusal to give in to this Israelite God, he finally says, yes, just go – BUT… who will be going with you? Is it just the men? Just a few families? Is it the women and children? In other words, he wanted to know who was going to stay behind to take care of his kingdom and keep him rich and happy?

Moses' answer is, ALL. All must go, all the captives, all the slaves. ALL!

This is the question and the offer to each of us today. Who is going?

Sadly, not everyone will go. Not everyone chooses to go. Many will never make the choice to leave the bondage of Egypt, to leave Pharaoh behind and step out into the unknown of freedom. Everyone gets to choose – but not everyone does.

Each of us know hundreds of people – some as friends, some as acquaintances, some as family, some as co-workers - and all, at one point, are enslaved to something. At some point in each life, each person must choose to move forward or to stay behind.

Many will not go with you.

How many people do you know who are still stuck in ruts of self-denial and harmful ways of living?

____

____

____

Do you understand that you cannot force them to choose to live differently?

____

____

____

Do you understand that you have to choose to move forward - with or without them?

____

____

____

Prayer for Day 13:

Father, today, I choose to move forward. I understand that many will not understand the choice I am making. Many of my friends will not move forward with me. I ask that You would allow Your Light and Your Love to shine through me each day. Let me become a beacon of hope to those who are watching me. Fill me with Your light and love and teach me how to become a blessing to those around me. Let the path You are leading me on, this journey I am on, be a pathway that others will want to follow. In Jesus' Name, Amen.

Scripture Reading for Day 13:

Exodus Chapter 10
Matthew 22:14

Day 13 Life Challenge Questions:

What bondage are you still choosing to live in when freedom is available?

Why are you still living in that bondage?

When will you choose to walk in freedom?

Can you describe how it would feel to be free from this bondage?

Day 14

Question: Have I not commanded you?

Joshua 1:9 "Have I not commanded you? Be strong and courageous. Do not be afraid, do not be discouraged, for the Lord your God will be with you wherever you go."

Moses has just died. The old ways are over, now what? Joshua was Moses' right-hand man. After Moses' death, Joshua is naturally the next in line to lead the people. But he is a little anxious and fearful and a bit nervous. He was probably asking himself how he could ever begin to fill Moses' shoes. He was probably asking himself if he had what it takes to be a leader of people. Could he step into something new and be a good leader and a good example?

Sometimes God needs to be blunt with us. We tend to become hard of hearing, and hard of believing. I like how God is blunt and forceful with Joshua at this point. He tells him (Joshua 1:1-2), "Moses my servant is dead. Now then, you and all of these people, get ready…"

God plainly tells him, the mourning period is over, it is time to move on, you take over, you lead. It is like God is telling him, you do it, its time. Right now.

Even though God is firm, He is also kind and in Joshua 1:5, He says, "…as I was with Moses, so I will be with you..." God, his Father, says to him, "Haven't I commanded you to be strong and courageous? Haven't I said, do not be afraid? Haven't I said, do not be discouraged?"

Joshua hears the word of the Lord, and he steps up and becomes the next great leader of the Israelites. It is Joshua who leads the people into the promised land of freedom.

God says the same to you today. He says, I see you. I know you. I know how strong you really are. Now go. Move forward and I will be with you, just as I have always been with My children.

Then God says, oh, and one more thing, this is how you will be successful and succeed: "Keep this Book of the Law always on your lips, meditate on it day and night…" (Joshua 1:8)

Are you in a place where you are fearful about moving forward?

____

____

____

____

Do you trust God when He says that He will be with you and help you?

____

____

____

Do you think you can step up and help lead one person? ______________

Two people? ______________________________

Many people? _____________________________

What is holding you back from being strong and courageous?

____

____

____

____

Are your fears or insecurities based on fact or thoughts?

____

____

____

Prayer for Day 14:

Father, today, I ask for strength and courage. Strength to continue moving forward, strength to overcome obstacles or setbacks, strength to train myself to love Your Word. I ask You to give me courage to face what is hard. Give me courage to overcome and move forward just like Joshua did. What was done in the past is finished, over. Give me strength and courage to step on, step up and step over. In Jesus' Name, Amen.

Scripture Reading for Day 14:

Joshua Chapter 1
Isaiah 40:29
Psalm 18:32

Day 14 Life Challenge Questions:

Do you truly believe God sees you and knows you?

Journal how you know this, write your testimony here with the details of how God found you.

Do you know what He is calling you to do? Journal it – write it down! Pen to paper!

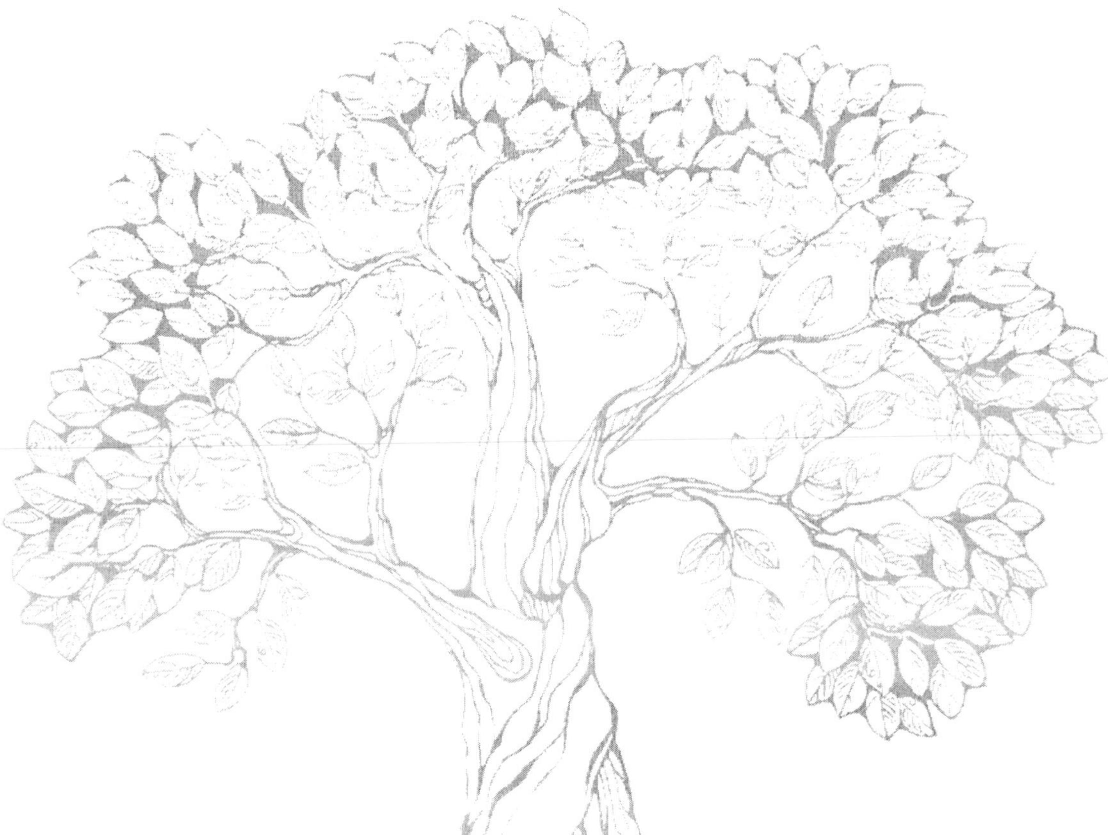

Day 15

Question: Why have I found favor in your eyes?

Ruth 2:10 "At this, she bowed down with her face to the ground. Why have I found such favor in your eyes that you notice me, a foreigner?"

I think we all ask this question at some point in our journey with God. His goodness is following us, He is blessing us, we feel refreshed and stronger today than we did yesterday. Yet, we question this goodness. Why God?

The why questions are usually tied to years of negative thinking and self-doubt. Why me? I am nobody. I am worthless. On and on and on the old tapes run through our heads.

Right now – push the STOP button on the why questions. Push the STOP button on the old tapes replaying in your mind.

YOU – yes, you, have found favor with God because YOU ARE HIS! You belong to Him. He loves you with an everlasting love and His desire is to show you how much He loves you.

The Father loves you so much that He will sometimes surprise you with little gifts. These little gifts from God will seem very small and insignificant to other people, but to you, it will have great significance. Great beauty. It will mean everything to you. This is God showing up in your life through the little things. It may come to you as a perfect sunset, or a beautiful flower, a wonderful piece of music, a simple verse or poem.

These little gifts from God could be anything, yet you will know it when you see it, *if you are looking*. Remember that God operates in a different realm than we do. He can reach down through the heavenlies and place the perfect little gift in your path at any moment, anytime, anywhere. It will be something special just for you.

Now we can ask God the "why" question, and He answers:

Because you are loved.
Because you are chosen.
Because you are mine.

He loves you! He loves you! He loves you!

Open your eyes and begin to watch for the little gifts of grace and beauty coming your way.

Do you have trouble with the concept that you are loved by your Heavenly Father? If so, why?

Have you recently experienced a small event that has made you catch your breath in awe? Did it surprise you? Did you recognize it as a gift from your Father? Describe it.

Prayer for Day 15:

Father, I thank You for these little gifts of favor that You send my way. Open my eyes so that I can see everything You are giving me. Thank You for loving me even when I am asking why. Thank You for loving me even when I couldn't see You or didn't know You. Open my eyes today to see in a new way, to see each gift that You place in my path, whether large or small. Thank You for thinking of me and showing me that You are there. In Jesus' Name, Amen.

Scripture Reading for Day 15:

Matthew 7:7-12
1 Corinthians, Chapter 2

Day 15 Life Challenge Questions:

Can you look back at your life and see God's hand? He has been there!

How has God orchestrated the events in your life that have brought you to this exact moment? Can you see a timeline with God's hand all over it?

Journal this timeline. Start with the events you can remember, no matter how small or how far back it goes. (Suggestion: if you struggle with remembering when God had His hand on you, start with the most recent little gift that God has given you, and then work backward from there.)

Day 16

Question: What do you see?

***Ezekiel 8:15*: "He said to me, do you see this, son of man…?"**

Ezekiel was one of the greatest prophets of his time and God used him mightily in many ways. One day, Ezekiel had a vision from God. He saw himself standing in front of the great temple in Jerusalem. The temple was the center of Jewish worship and was supposed to be a holy place dedicated to the Lord.

In the vision, God took Ezekiel to one of the walls inside the temple. There was a small hole in the wall that allowed Ezekiel to look inside and see what was going on deep inside the temple, behind closed doors.

Behind those walls, behind those closed doors, it was dark and things were taking place on the inside of the temple that outsiders couldn't see. Questionable things, strange things, harmful things. God shines His light through the hole in the wall and asks Ezekiel to tell Him what he sees in there.

We all have walls built up around our hearts and around the deepest parts of us. Walls of stone and brick that we have erected over the years to protect us and help us feel safe. These walls have doors, and the doors are locked – shut up tight, from the inside.

God, our Father, asks us to peek through the little hole in the wall of our heart. He begins to ask us to tell Him what we see. He asks us to take a look in order to pry the doors open so that He can shine His light in there. As He begins to shine His light on what lies deep down inside, the lies, the doubts, the fears, the uncertainty, the failure, the what ifs… His light begins to reveal the truth.

God sent Jesus here to earth to shine the light of His truth, His Kingdom, His power on the darkness of "us." It is His light that hands us the key to unlock the doors to the walls that hold us. It is His light that hands us the shovel and says – start digging through that wall – with Me. Don't go there without Me. Jesus says, I died to set you free, so let Me take you through the walls to freedom. One by one, door by door, stone by stone, brick by brick, the walls will come down and His light will shine through.

Today might be the day to start peeking through that wall. Or it might be next week, or next month or next year. When the time is right, allow the light of His love to go with you.

What do you think Jesus sees when He looks through that little hole in the wall around your heart?

____

____

____

____

What do you see when you look through that little hole in the wall around your heart?

____

____

____

____

Prayer for Day 16:

Father, the walls I have built around me to protect me – are huge and thick. But I am tired of living in the shadows. Help me today to trust You enough to go there with me. Show me how to do this. Today, I ask You to heal my brokenness, to heal my hurts, heal my loss, heal my heart. I want to be free. I want to be whole. I want to be the "me" that You created me to be. In Jesus' Name, Amen.

Scripture Reading for Day 16:

Ezekiel 8:1-13
Isaiah 45:2
Luke 4:16-19

Day 16 Life Challenge Questions:

Are there any questionable activities going on inside the walls of your heart right now, such as: jealousy, unforgiveness, anger, shame. Are you hiding anything that needs to be exposed by the light of His love?

Can you be honest with God? Yes, you can be honest with Him because you cannot turn His love away from you no matter what you have done, or are doing.
He wants you. All of you!

Day 17

Question: What did you hear?

1 Samuel 3:10 "The Lord came and stood there, calling as at the other times, Samuel! Samuel! Then Samuel said, speak for your servant is listening."

Samuel was just a child when he heard the voice of the Lord speaking to him. At first, he didn't understand what he was hearing or who was speaking, but his mentor and friend told him to listen carefully, and reply in this way: "I am here." Why?

When God speaks, we acknowledge, we answer, even if we are unsure.

Do you believe that God speaks to his children? If we go all the way back to the beginning, back to the garden of Eden, back to Adam and back to Eve, we see that God's desire was to have fellowship with His children, His creation. He walked among them and talked with them.

Genesis 3:8 tells us: "Then the man and his wife heard the sound of Lord God as He was walking in the garden in the cool of the day…"

God, just strolling through the paradise He had created with His kids, His children. That was His intent, perfect fellowship and perfect friendship with His creation. But mankind chose otherwise. Man chose to go his own way and step away from God. Yet, God still pursued them. He still called out to them. Even today, He calls out to us to return to Him, to come back into fellowship with Him through His son, Jesus. God sent Jesus to restore that broken fellowship. Jesus says to us in John 10:27: "My sheep (my children) listen to my voice, I know them, and they follow me."

The sheep hear the voice of the Shepherd. When did we stop hearing? When did we stop listening? Did we ever hear? Or was the voice of the world screaming louder?

To hear the voice of the Lord our God, our Father, our Shepherd, we must quiet ourselves long enough to hear.

Isaiah 30:15 tells us how: "This is what the Sovereign Lord, the Holy One of Israel says: In repentance and rest is your salvation, in quietness and trust is your strength…"

Strength and confidence come through quietness.

Getting quiet in this busy world can be difficult. In order to grow and mature in our spiritual walk, we need to practice the art of "quiet time."

Find time to get quiet before the Lord, even if it is just for a few minutes. If you experience stress or conflict or confusion in your day, stop, and rest. Close your eyes and get quiet.

Without quiet time before the Lord, we will not grow.

How difficult is it for you to set aside quiet time in your day?

____

____

If you find this hard to do, start small. Make a point right here and now to begin a new daily habit of quiet time. Make a commitment right now. What do you think you can manage? You can be honest here, God knows.

Five minutes? Fifteen minutes? Half an hour?

____

____

Prayer for Day 17:

Quiet time? Oh, Lord, this is another hard thing for me to do. I have so much going on right now, so many things going through my head right now. This seems impossible. But, I long to hear from You and walk with You and I long to know more about You and Your ways. Help me today to begin to set aside a few minutes of quiet time, for You. Speak to my heart each day as I learn to rest in You. In Jesus' Name, Amen.

Scripture Reading for Day 17

1 Samuel, Chapter 3

Day 17 Life Challenge Questions:

Why does God want to spend time with you? (Remember, God loves relationship! God is relational!)

How can you have a relationship with anyone if you never spend time together?

How do you get to know someone if you never spend time with them?

What do you want with God and what do you want from God?

Day 18

Question: How long will you waver between two opinions?

1 Kings 18:21 "Elijah went before the people and said, How long will you waver between two opinions? If the Lord is God, follow Him; but if Baal is god, follow him."

Back and forth, side to side, front to back… we tend to bend and lean toward what we want to hear or be at any particular moment; good, bad, right, wrong, or otherwise.

Living "in the moment" is a selfish and harmful way to live. This type of living calls upon us to satisfy the desires of our flesh and do whatever we feel like doing at the moment. Ask anyone who has been down that road, it only leads to destruction.

It is time to make a stand against back and forth, bending and leaning. It is time to stand and be firm in what you know to be true.

Ephesians 4-14 says: "Then we will no longer be infants, tossed back and forth by the waves, and blown here and there by every wind of teaching, and by the cunning and craftiness of people in their deceitful scheming."

Going back and forth and wavering is something that infants and toddlers do. They are young and vulnerable, and untrained.

We are encouraged to grow up and mature in our walk with God. We are not to remain as infants and toddlers.

James 1:4-8 says: "Let perseverance finish its work so that you may be mature and complete, not lacking anything. If any of you lacks wisdom, you should ask God, who gives generously to all without finding fault, and it will be given to you. But, when you ask, you must believe and not doubt, because the one who doubts is like a wave of the sea, blown and tossed by the wind. That person should not expect to receive anything from the Lord. Such a person is double-minded and unstable in all they do."

It is clear that God does not want us to be "double-minded," or wishy-washy and unstable. He says to ask and believe and stand firm on what you believe.

Stand. Stand firm. Don't waver. Don't go back and forth.

Luke 21:19 tells us to "Stand firm and you will win life."

1 Corinthians 15:58 says: "Therefore my dear brothers and sisters, stand firm. Let nothing move you..."

Ephesians 6:14 says: "Stand firm then, with the belt of truth buckled around your waist…"

Galatians 5:1 says: "It is for freedom that Christ has set us free. Stand firm then, and do not let yourselves be burdened again by a yoke of slavery."

It is time to make a decision to stand firm. It is time to make a decision to not waver or go back and forth.

Stand firm in what you believe.
Stand firm in what you know.
Stand firm and do not bend, do not waver, do not give in.

Prayer for Day 18:

Today, Father, I make a choice to stand firm in the knowledge of what You are showing me to be true. I don't understand all of it yet, but I am willing to learn. I am trusting that You will show me what I need to understand as I grow in You. I don't want to be pulled in two directions any more. So today, help me not to waver between two opinions, or go back and forth in my beliefs and my wants. Help me to stand firm in what Your Word says about me. Help me today to plant my feet on the solid rock foundation of the truth of Your Word. In Jesus' Name, Amen.

Scripture Reading for Day 18

1 Kings 18:16-24
Ephesians 4:14-15
James 1:1-8

Day 18 Life Challenge Questions:

How long have you gone back and forth between your old familiar patterns and a new way of living?

What were your old familiar patterns? Can you define them?

What new lifestyle patterns would you like to create?

Day 19

Question: What are you doing here?

1 Kings 19:9 "There he went into a cave and spent the night. And the word of the Lord came to him: what are you doing here Elijah?"

There are times when even the prophets and the great men of God got tired, weary and afraid. They too sometimes wanted to run away and hide.

We are no different.

In the reference above we see that the prophet Elijah was tired and weary after months of traveling and delivering the Word of God to the people. Because of the words he spoke many people hated him. One day he just had enough and wandered away and found a dark cave to hide in. The perfect place to escape and sleep.

But God knew his heart. God saw him and He called out to him, "Elijah, what are you doing?" In other words, don't give up, don't quit.

Immediately Elijah responds with words like: I am just so tired, I am exhausted, I am afraid, this is too hard. I can't do this.

God tells him: "Enough. Go stand in My presence and I will show you My glory." In other words, God said to him, I know you are weary, but stand in My presence and let My glory fill you so that you can carry on and move forward in the purpose I have set before you.

Elijah's life was full of purpose, and he had work to do. He had people to help and people to teach. God had plans for Elijah and work that only Elijah could accomplish.

This is also true of you. Your life is full of purpose and you have work to do and people to help.

God was kind of asking Elijah how long he planned to hang out in the dark cave of hiding. Finally God told him, enough is enough. Seek Me. Then move forward in what I need you to accomplish.

We too must decide to come out of our self-made caves of hiding and approach God. We need to let His glory and light shine on us, heal us, refresh us, and restore us – so that we can move forward in our purpose. Just as Elijah was called by God for a specific purpose, we too are called by God to do something more, or to be something more.

How are you still living within your own cave of hiding?

____

____

____

Is it time for you to emerge and step into the light of God's glory?

____

____

Prayer for Day 19:

No more hiding Lord. Today I choose to step out of the cave of darkness and hiding into Your marvelous light. Let each day from here forward be filled with more of Your light and glory. I ask that You would begin to open my eyes to all the possibilities that are before me. Help me understand the purposes and plans that You have for my life. In Jesus' Name, Amen.

Scripture Reading for Day 19:

1 Kings 19:3-15
Jeremiah 29:11-14

Day 19 Life Challenge Questions:

God has a specific plan and purpose for the rest of your life. Can you begin to define this purpose and plan?

If you are struggling with the concept of a purpose for your life, think about this: your purpose in life usually comes from something you are passionate about. What are some of the things that you love? Start making a list today. Think outside the scope of your family and beyond the routine of daily life. Think big! (Examples: art, mountains, travel, farming, woodworking, nature...)

Is there anything in your life that you feel like you would die for?

Day 20

Question: Who will go for us?

Isaiah 6:8 "Then I heard the voice of the Lord saying, whom shall I send? And who will go for us...?"

Nothing gets accomplished by God on the earth without people. We weren't created to just simply sit around and do nothing.

We were created to rule and to reign on earth. But what exactly does that mean? What were we created to rule over?

Genesis 2:15 says, "The Lord God took the man and put him in the garden of Eden to work it, and take care of it."

We were made to take care of the earth, to tend it, nurture it, cause it to grow and produce and flourish. We are far from that in our current lifetime.

We were created and designed to reign, to have power. Over what? Over everything on earth. Over the creatures and every living thing. Genesis 1:26 says: *"Then God said, Let us make mankind in our image, in our likeness, so that they may rule over the fish in the sea and the birds in the sky, over the livestock and over all the wild animals, and over all the creatures that move along the ground."* Genesis 2:15 says: *"The Lord God took the man and put him in the Garden of Eden to work it and take care of it."*

Man was to rule and reign and tend the earth and take care of it. What happened? *Adam made the choice to go his own way, to do his own thing*, to disregard what God had said and to make his own decisions. He made a choice to "self-govern" which led not only to his own destruction, but the destruction of all of mankind. This is where sin enters the earth, and as they say, "all hell breaks loose." Man gave up his right to rule and reign, and turned the earth over to the enemy, to Satan and his kingdom.

Hardship and evil enter the earth at this point, and it is never the same. This earth, as it is today, is not what God intended. Choosing to live outside of what God intended allowed the enemy to take over and begin unleashing darkness, death, and destruction. The enemy is the one who causes chaos, death and destruction, not God.

The good news is that God always had a plan for redemption. Jesus, the Son, was sent to redeem mankind and win back what was lost. He was sent to restore what we lost in the garden, which was, light, love, life, ruling and reigning.

Jesus came to earth, and brought back God's Kingdom and plan for man. Through His teachings and His lifestyle, He showed us how to overcome darkness. Through His death on the cross, and His resurrection from death, He showed us how to walk in freedom.

As Jesus was teaching in the synagogue one day he read from the book of Isaiah, and then he told the people: I have come for *this purpose* – to proclaim good news, to heal the broken hearted, to set the captives free, to release those who are prisoners locked up in caves of darkness, to comfort those who are sad and to provide for those who grieve.

Wow. That is the whole point of restoration! To restore what was lost.

Jesus came and conquered death so that we might have eternal life. He conquered the enemy to set us free from ourselves, and from the grip the enemy has over us. Jesus had a purpose and a job to do here on earth, just like we have a purpose and a job to do.

Jesus came for restoration and to reign as King of kings and Lord of lords. He came to remove power from the enemy and give it back to us, to mankind. He passes that power on to us, His children, His sheep, His followers. We are to share this knowledge and this freedom with others on the earth.

Yet, Jesus asks the same question that God asked in Isaiah 6:8,

"Who will go for us? Who will go to the lost and the hurting and help to set them free?"

Not everyone chooses to step out into what God calls them to do.

Thousands of years ago the prophet Isaiah could see how great the needs of mankind were, and his response to God's call was, "here I am, send me."

We rule and reign in this life by answering the call of God. To answer the call means that we choose to be led by the Spirit of God, we choose to allow God to shape us and mold us into what He needs us to be, and we choose to hear the call to reign over evil in this world. We choose to do what we can do to help others. It is a choice.

When God asks, who will I send? What will your choice be?

____

____

____

____

Prayer for Day 20:

Father, today, I understand that the need to help others is great. I look around and I see so many hurting people. Open my eyes to the needs of others and help me begin to reach out to them, even if its in very small ways. Help me to see Your children, Your people, the way that You do, with eyes full of compassion and love. In Jesus' Name, Amen.

Scripture Reading for Day 20:

Isaiah 61:1-2
Genesis 1:26-30
Genesis 2:15-17
Luke 4:14-20

Day 20 Life Challenge Questions:

What has God called you to do?

If you do not know the answer to this question, it is time to stop, sit with the Lord and ask Him what He is calling you to do!

How can you, yes you, help restore His Kingdom here on this earth? What does that look like for you?

Day 21

Question: Why are you here?

Esther 4:14 "…and who knows but that you have come to royal position for such a time as this?"

Esther was a young Jewish girl born into captivity. Her people had been taken captive by the Persians and were moved to a foreign country to be used as slaves.

Esther was young and she was also beautiful. She was beautiful on the outside and beautiful on the inside. She loved God and was faithful to Him. After her parents died, her uncle Mordecai raised her in a traditional Jewish family, even though they lived among people of another culture.

Esther's beauty was noticed by many people, including the King of Persia, King Xerxes, who happened to be looking for a new queen. The king orders all of the young single women in the kingdom to be brought into the palace where they would live and be trained in the ways of a palace socialite. Then he would choose one of them for his queen.

Among the hundreds of young girls the king had to choose from, he chose Esther.

This young Jewish girl is promoted from captivity to the palace in just a few months' time. Because of Esther's loving heart, she is a light to all of those who are around her – she is noticed.

But, danger lurks around the corner and soon the lives of Esther's people are threatened. An enemy wants to wipe them out and destroy the Jewish people.

Uncle Mordecai tells Esther that she must go before the king and ask for the Jewish people to be saved from harm. But nobody goes before the king unless he calls for them, and Esther has not been summoned to appear before the king.

Time is running out for the Jewish people and Uncle Mordecai says to Esther, you must go to the king for us, "*who knows but that you have come to royal position for such a time as this?*"

Esther spends time praying and fasting and then she takes a risk. She approached the king, the king sees her and allows her to come before him, and she is able to save her people from annihilation.

This was Esther's God given purpose while she was here on earth. To save her people.

She was born where she was, when she was, moved to a different country when she did, and then moved to the palace to be able to save her people when it was time. She heard the call when it came, and she responded.

Each of us have a God-given purpose while we are here on this earth. We may not know what it is at this moment, but when it is presented to you, by God your Father, you will know. Then the choice will be yours, to rise up and answer the call, to see to the need presented to you and move upon it – or to remain safe and stay hidden.

You are here, right now, in this point in history, "for such a time as this."

You are needed. You are wanted. You are stronger than you know. Be watching and waiting for your "such a time as this."

Do you realize that you are where you are today, because God needs you right where you are.

God has a specific purpose in mind for you, and you alone.

Can you make a list of some of the people in Scripture who were set apart for a specific task?

____

____

Prayer for Day 21:

Father, I feel that I am too young, or too old, or too shy, or too afraid to step out and do anything right now. I ask for Your help. Help me to "see" myself as strong and confident, like You see me. If a young girl like Esther can rise up and help a whole group of people, I can too. I ask that You would mold me and shape me and make me into a person of integrity and strength that can be used for Your Kingdom and Your work here on this earth. Help me to be willing and able to answer the call, whenever and however it comes my way. In Jesus' Name, Amen.

Scripture Reading for Day 21:

Esther Chapter 4

Day 21 Life Challenge Questions:

Have ever wondered why you are here, or why you are even alive?

Esther presented herself to her king after she prepared herself. She prepared her body, her mind and her spirit to go before her king. How are you preparing yourself to go before your King?

How will you present yourself to God?

Day 22

Question: Can you fathom the mysteries of God?

Job 42:1-3 "Then Job replied to the Lord, I know that You can do all things; no plan of yours can be thwarted. You asked, Who is this that obscures my counsel without knowledge? Surely, I spoke of things I did not understand, things too wonderful for me to know."

There is a certain amount of mystery to our God, our Heavenly Father. Who He is, how He operates, how He thinks, how He responds.

Unless we accept the mysteries of God, the unanswerable questions that we have about Him, we may never be able to move forward in absolute trust and faith in Him.

Jesus told us that we needed to be able to see things like little children do. They see and they accept, without having to know all the answers. (Matthew 18:3)

In our "humanness" we have limited thinking and understanding, the longer we walk with God and the longer that we study His Word, the more understanding we receive.

If you tend to be a more analytical type of person, you will have a hard time accepting that "God is." God is this; or God is that; God can do this; or God can do that; because you are unable to understand it.

We have to let go of the constant analysis and think like a child, not act like a child, but think like one. We need to be able to accept the wonders and awe and endless possibilities that exist with God.

He is more than enough. He is everywhere, He is everything that we need Him to be. Begin to have confidence in that truth alone.

Then, seek Him. In Matthew 6:33, Jesus tells us: "but seek first His Kingdom and His righteousness, and all these things will be given to you as well."

And in Luke 11:10, Jesus said, "For everyone who asks receives, the one who seeks finds, and to the one who knocks, the door will be opened."

Ask, seek, knock. These words are verbs. They require action on our part. They require us to do *something*.

Many people give up and turn away from the Lord because they just don't understand Him and His Kingdom. They just don't understand all of the mysteries of God. Jesus himself tells us that the information will come to those who knock, to those who diligently seek for the answers.

Read, study, pray and the things that you need to understand will be revealed to you. Don't give up. Don't turn back. Let your heart and mind become "like a little child" and take in all the awe and wonder of our marvelous God and Father.

ASK ***SEEK*** ***KNOCK***

What are some of the unanswerable questions about God causing you to struggle?

____

____

____

Why is it hard for you to accept that some of the qualities of God, and the attributes of God will always remain a mystery?

____

____

____

____

Prayer for Day 22:

Oh, Lord, I have so many questions! There is so much that is a mystery to me. Help me not to have to understand everything about You right now, just help me to believe. I trust Father, that as I seek You and Your Kingdom, that You will reveal Your truths to me. I hand over to You today, all of my unanswerable questions, and believe that what I need to know, You will show me at the proper time. Trust, trust, trust. I trust You now Father. In Jesus' Name, Amen.

Scripture Reading for Day 22

Matthew 18:1-9

Day 22 Life Challenge Questions:

What is the biggest mystery of God that you are struggling with right now?

Share it with Him, be honest with your struggle. Journal your questions, then be on the lookout for the answers. He wants you to know Him intimately!

Day 23

Question: Who gave you wisdom and understanding?

Job 38:36 (NKJV) "Who has put wisdom in the mind? Or who has given understanding to the heart?"

In the beginning God…. back to the beginning, back to the garden, back to the birth of mankind on this earth. God states His intent for us in Genesis 1:26, "*Then God said, let us make mankind in our image, in our likeness, so that they may rule…*"

God speaks, and He uses the term "us," plural, more than one. God speaks on behalf of the three, Father God, Son Jesus and Holy Spirit. He says, let us create this creature, this "mankind" and let him be like us, Father, Son and Holy spirit.

You see, we were created in the "likeness" or image of God Himself. We were created in the likeness, or image, of those who live in the Heavenly Spiritual realm. God breathed His own breath, His own "life" into the first man. His plan was for that man, and all men and women after him, to become His family, His children.

All that God was and is and ever will be, was deposited into the spiritual DNA of the first man. Knowledge, wisdom, love and success were part of that DNA. God placed it there.

Free will and choice are also part of what God deposited into man, and man chose to step away from God. That choice altered God's plan and desire for His children. Adam, in his perfect state of being, knew no evil, no hatred, no hardship, until he chose to believe the lies presented to him by his enemy.

Free will and choice are a result of wanting to control our own circumstances and make our own decisions, apart from God and without God's advice.

Adam made the decision to go his own way and do his own thing, and all of us have been doing the same thing ever since.

Adam chose to step away from God and immediately he begins to experience all of the negative effects of his choice. He begins to feel sorrow, loss, shame, heartache, loneliness and hardship. This is not what God intended for us.

But God, in His perfect wisdom and knowledge, has a plan for restoration and redemption. Thousands of years later, the Son of God, steps into the earth as a human child. He came to restore God's original intent, He came to repair what had been damaged through Adam, He came to give us life and show us how to, once again, live within God's wonderful Kingdom.

Every person on the face of the earth is seeking to "be restored." We are all looking for something that was lost, and we look for it in a thousand different ways: *self-indulgence, greed, religion, sex, shopping, power, control, cars, drugs, houses, money, relationships.*

People are broken. Jesus came to help us find our way back to wholeness.

God says to us: I have created you, and I have given you My Son for restoration, and I have given you wisdom and understanding so that you can find your way back to Me.

When man gave in to his own desires in the garden, what is your understanding of what we lost there?

____

____

____

____

____

Prayer for Day 23:

Oh, Father, I am truly in need of restoration. Restore my mind today. Restore my heart today, restore my thoughts today, restore my desires today. Father, I give You permission today to hit the "reset" button in my life and restore me to wholeness in You. Let me walk in Your ways, not my own. Let me talk in Your ways, not my own. Let me think and act in Your ways, not my own. Father, I ask that You would restore me right now and fill me with Your wisdom and Your knowledge. Fill me with Your love and light and with Your perfect peace and joy. In Jesus' Name, Amen.

Scripture Reading for Day 23:

Genesis 3:22-24
John 10:9-11

Day 23 Life Challenge Questions:

Give God a chance with your heart. He has been waiting a long time for you to come to Him with your true heart. What have you personally lost and would like to have restored? Name it. Be completely honest with God, He can handle your emotions and your desires.

Day 24

Question: What does God want from me?

Micah 6:8 "He has shown you, o mortal, what is good. And what does the Lord require of you? To act justly and to love mercy and to walk humbly with your God."

This question comes directly from God Himself directed to His people, His children.

It's a great question. What does God require of us? What does God need from us? What does God need from you?

God's answer to the prophet Micah went like this: here's what I need my people to do; they need to act justly (truthfully) all the time. I need them to be filled with mercy for others, just as I am filled with mercy for them, all of the time; and I need them to live and walk humbly before Me, at all times.

The Message translation of Micah 6:8 makes it even clearer for us: "But He's already made it plain how to live, what to do, what God is looking for in men and women. It's quite simple, do what is fair and just to your neighbor, be compassionate and loyal in your love, and don't take yourself too seriously, take God seriously."

Jesus came to earth as our example. He showed us how to live life the way God desires. Jesus taught us to be honest and fair in our dealings with others (Matthew 18:21-35). Jesus was full of mercy and compassion for others (Luke 23:32-34). Are you??

Jesus' example to us was to love everyone and have compassion for everyone, no matter who they are or where they come from. (Luke 10:25-37).

God spoke His desires for how we should live our lives throughout the Old Testament. Jesus came and literally walked it out to show us how to do it in the New Testament. Jesus' followers and apostles continued to walk and live the way Jesus taught them, until they left this earth. We are called to do the same.

Read today's passages of scripture to see the examples that Jesus gave us and then ask yourself:

How do I allow mercy, forgiveness and compassion to be my compass each day?

____

____

____

When do I reach out to others with some type of help or support when I see a need?

____

____

____

How often am I able to give a simple word of encouragement to those who are weary?

____

____

Do I feel the need to let others see the good things I am doing, or am I satisfied with walking quietly with God, allowing Him to guide me in the things I need to do?

____

____

____

____

Prayer for Day 24:

Father, sometimes it is really hard for me to be humble and quiet. It can be so hard to love others when they are annoying, irritating or mean. But I do want to learn how to walk, think and act like Jesus at all times. Help me today to be humble and quiet before you. Lead me today and every day in the direction You want me to go. Help me to always understand what You want to me to do and say to be a blessing to those around me. In Jesus' Name, Amen.

Scripture Reading for Day 24:

Luke 10:25-37
Luke 23:32-34
Matthew 18:21-35

Day 24 Life Challenge Questions:

What specific thing is God asking of you? It could be a habit He is asking you to let go of, or a person He wants you to forgive, or a situation He wants you to walk away from.

Spend time with the Lord today and allow Him to speak His heart's desire to you.

Describe how you think you could walk humbly before God.

Day 25

Question: Are you hiding?

1 Samuel 10:21-22 (NASB) "Then he brought the tribe of Benjamin forward by its families, and the Matrite family was selected by lot. And Saul the son of Kish was selected by lot; but when they looked for him, he could not be found. Therefore they inquired further of the Lord, has the man (Saul) come here yet? And the Lord said, Behold, he is hiding himself among the baggage."

Hiding. We all do it. Some of us are better at it than others.

Some of us have backpacks filled with the garbage of our past, and others have tons of baggage that they have become pretty good at hiding behind. Some of us have tote bags, grocery bags and three or four suitcases filled with the stuff that holds us hostage.

Some of us love our baggage. It gives us a wall to hide behind, just like Saul did in the verses above.

Saul was called by God to become the first king over Israel. He was filled with God-given greatness and he was chosen for a specific purpose. His life was needed, his valor was needed, his strength was needed. But when it came time for him to step up to rule and reign, he remained hidden. The voices within the baggage cried out to Saul and said, *you aren't, you can't, you will never will...*

The baggage in Saul's life was heavy enough to hide the truth of who he really was.

No matter how big or small our baggage is, it weighs us down, slowing our progress, hiding who we were designed by God to be.

So, the question is, what do we do with our baggage? How do we unpack it and throw out the trash and move forward?

Proverbs 20:5 (NASB) says, *"The plan in the heart of a person is like deep water, but a person of understanding draws it out."*

Sometimes we need to seek the wisdom and counsel of others to help us unpack our bags. People with knowledge and insight can help us start pulling out the "stuff" we have packed away for years like: shame, guilt, anger, hatred, envy, remorse, loneliness…

We were not created to hide. We were created to live and rule and reign with Jesus! (John 10:10)

How much baggage are you hiding behind? How much baggage are you carrying around that is weighing you down and holding you back?

____

____

____

____

Explain how you believe that there is greatness and purpose placed within you by God.

____

____

____

When is it time for you to allow that greatness to arise?

____

____

____

____

Prayer for Day 25:

Father, today, I declare that I no longer want to hide among the baggage of my life. I ask for Your help to guide me in tearing down and throwing away every bag that holds me hostage and holds me back. Jesus, shine Your light on the dark places and reveal Your truth to my heart today. I believe greatness, purpose and holiness lie within me and today I say, arise! In Jesus' Name, Amen.

Scripture Reading for Day 25:

1 Samuel 10:17-26

Day 25 Life Challenge Questions:

Can you name your baggage? Your deepest hurts?

Who has hurt you?

How have they hurt you?

Words can be the deadliest weapon. What words have wounded you?

All of this "baggage" must be thrown down at the feet of Jesus! Allow Him to give you complete freedom, that is His desire for you! FREEDOM! No hiding ever again!

Day 26

Question: Does my life have value?

Matthew 6:26 "Look at the birds of the air; they do not sow or reap or store away in barns, and yet your heavenly Father feeds them. Are you not much more valuable than they?"

Value is something more than what you can see, touch and feel. Value is beauty and depth; an asset, a need, worth, quality.

Birds have value for what they are; beauty in flight, simplicity in lifestyle, the sweet songs pouring forth from within them.

God placed the ability to be a bird, within the bird. Their lives are fragile and short lived, yet God says that they are valuable in his eye. Not one of them falls to the ground without the Father knowing about it. (Matthew 10:29).

Even the life of a sparrow holds value and purpose. All of God's creation has value.

Flowers hold the same sense of fragile beauty. They are here for a season, bursting forth in color and drama just to brighten our world.

If flowers and sparrows are precious and valuable to our Father, then how much more valuable are you?

All of us were created by God to be vessels, to be carriers of His beauty and His strength, His thoughts and His intents. We were born to become His glory carriers. We were born to bring light into this world, not darkness.

Oh! We feel so far from that at times!

The longer we walk with the Lord, and learn about Him and His ways, the closer we get to becoming like Him.

2 Corinthians 3:18 tells us: *"And we all, who with unveiled faces contemplate the Lord's glory, are being transformed into His image with ever increasing glory, which comes from the Lord, who is the Spirit."*

We must understand that we are in a process of renewal. All the "old ways" and old habits are being replaced with "new ways." New ways of living, new ways of being, new ways of thinking, new ways of reacting.

God deposits His attributes and qualities within us, and we become His vessels designed to carry His beauty, His strength and His glory into this hurting world.

Every time we let go of some of our old ways and move forward in God's new ways, we make room within ourselves to allow His glory to invade us.

God sees every sparrow, every bird, every flower, every tree, every animal and every person. He sees you. He sees your value and your worth and His desire is for you to be one of His glory carriers.

Repeat after me: "I am of great value to my Heavenly Father. I am loved. I am needed. I am destined to be one of His glory carriers."

Do you believe that your life has value?

____

____

____

Can you describe some of the qualities and attributes of God?

____

____

____

If you believe that you are created in God's image and His likeness and that those qualities live within you, can you name them?

____

____

____

Prayer for Day 26:

Oh Father! Sometimes it is so hard for me to see the value in myself. I tend to see the mistakes and the failures, and not the light and the value that You placed within me. Today, show me and remind me, as only You can, just how valuable I am to You. Help me to empty myself of the old ways and allow myself to be filled with Your new ways. Thank You that You find me valuable. Thank You that You need me. Thank You that You love me. In Jesus' Name, Amen.

Scripture Reading for Day 26:

Psalm 17:8
Matthew 6:25-30
2 Corinthians 3:18

Day 26 Life Challenge Questions:

How many "I am" statements can you write down? (Example: I am a child of God, John 1:2). Search the Word of God for yourself and find the truth of who you really are, make a list and write it down. Pen to paper!

Describe what you think it means to be a glory carrier for God:

Day 27

Question: Do you want to get well?

John 5:2-6 "Now there is in Jerusalem near the Sheep Gate, a pool, which in Aramaic is called Bethesda and which is surrounded by five covered colonnades. Here a great number of disabled people used to lie – the blind, the lame, the paralyzed. One who was there had been an invalid for thirty-eight years. When Jesus saw him lying there and learned that he had been in this condition for a long time, he asked him, do you want to get well?"

Do you want to get well? This seems like a strange question. Who doesn't want to be well? No one wants to be sick, ill or under the weather.

Jesus was in Jerusalem walking through the village and happened to go to the Pool of Bethesda. There He saw many people who were ill and suffering, but one man stood out to Him. This man had been an invalid for most of his life, living on the streets close to the pool and begging for handouts. This man felt sorry for himself day after day, year after year. Thirty eight years to be exact! That is a long time to live in despair.

The Pool of Bethesda was a popular place at that time. It was the local water reservoir for the town. Many who were blind, lame and sick sat by this pool every day, waiting and watching, hoping that something would happen to change their lives.

Occasionally the water would start bubbling, and they believed that if you were the first person to get into the pool when the water bubbled, you would be healed. Now, if you are paralyzed and have to drag yourself to get around, it would be almost impossible to get to the water before anyone else. The paralyzed man watched many others get into the water before him. And so he sat, day after day, week after week, year after year... until Jesus shows up.

Jesus sees this man, He sees his condition, He understands his despair, yet He asks him the question, *"do you want to get well?"*

In other words, is this really what you want? Immediately the paralyzed man starts making excuses for why he is still sick and paralyzed. He doesn't have anyone to help him get to the pool when it is bubbling, he can't walk, he isn't fast enough or strong enough…

The man doesn't answer Jesus' question, he just starts making excuses. But Jesus sees the heart of this man, the value within this man, He sees past his excuses.

Jesus calls him out of his self-pity and says: "Enough! Pick up your mat and walk."

Jesus gives him an order - pick up your mat! Get busy, do something, take possession of your healing, make it happen by doing what it takes to get well and to be healed. No more wishing, no more excuses.

It takes action and work and movement to get well, no matter what it is we need to get well from.

It is time for us to pick up our "mats of excuse." Our mats of resting. Our mats of resisting. It is time to pick them up, throw them out and move forward! Let's get up and get busy!

You are needed and Jesus has a plan for your life!

Have you found yourself making any excuses lately? If so, what are they?

____

____

____

____

____

Are there certain steps you know you need to take in order to bring about changes in your circumstances? What are those steps?

What is holding you back?

Prayer for Day 27:

Father, today I arise from my mat of excuses and from my mat of "what could have been or should have been," and I choose to do the work and get busy working on "me." No more delays! Thank you for taking my hand and walking me through the "walking it out" process. I call upon Your divine help, Your divine power, Your divine strength to overcome the "me" I used to be. In Jesus' Name, Amen.

Scripture Reading for Day 27:

John 5:1-9

Day 27 Life Challenge Questions:

What is it that you want Jesus to heal? Are there physical things, mental things, emotional things or spiritual things that you want the great Healer to heal?

Take each thing and lay it before Jesus. Ask yourself, am I willing to do what He asks of me to receive the healing I desire?

What is Jesus asking you to do?

Day 28

Question: Can you pick grapes off of thornbushes?

Matthew 7:16-17 "By their fruit you will recognize them. Do people pick grapes from thornbushes, or figs from thistles? Likewise, every good tree bears good fruit, but a bad tree bears bad fruit."

According to Genesis 1:1-13, God created vegetation, trees and grasses on the third day. Within every type and form of vegetation, tree or grass, God placed a seed, the ability to reproduce itself and multiply and spread.

Trees bear fruit with a seed inside that has the capacity to reproduce another tree. Berry bushes bear fruit that contains seeds that can multiply and reproduce more berry bushes. Grasses too bear fruit in their own way by blooming and producing seeds.

Every seed that is produced and planted within the right environment (such as good soil, water and sunlight) has the ability to reproduce itself over and over.

In Genesis 1:28, after creating mankind, the Bible says that "*God blessed them and said to them, be fruitful and increase in number, fill the earth and subdue it...*"

Bearing fruit and increasing in number are two totally different things.

"Bearing fruit" means to <u>reproduce</u> or replicate or release, <u>what is inside of you.</u>

"Increasing in number" refers to multiplying and expanding.

Humans, just like the vegetation and plants, were created by God to "bear fruit."

The Father deposits His Spirit within us when we are re-created, or re-born spiritually into His Kingdom. At this point, we are to begin taking on the attributes of God's Spirit in our life.

Galatians 5:22 tells us exactly what those attributes are. They are referred to as the "fruit of the Spirit."

"But the fruit of the Spirit is love, joy, peace, forbearance (patience), kindness, goodness, faithfulness, gentleness and self-control. Against such things there is no law."

This is the kind of fruit we are to show in our lives: love, joy, peace, patience, kindness, goodness, faithfulness and self control!

Jesus further explains this concept in Matthew 7:15-20 (AMP):

"Beware of false prophets (teachers) who come to you dressed as sheep (appearing gentle and innocent), but inwardly are ravenous wolves. By their fruit you will recognize them (that is, by their contrived doctrine and self-focus). Do people pick grapes from thornbushes or figs from thistles? Even so, every healthy tree bears good fruit, but the unhealthy tree bears bad fruit. A good tree cannot bear bad fruit, nor can a bad tree bear good fruit. Every tree that does not bear good fruit is cut down and thrown into the fire. Therefore, by their fruit you will recognize them (as false prophets)."

Jesus is teaching His followers how to recognize the difference between good people and bad people. He refers to people as "trees" in these verses, and these trees, or people, produce fruit that is either good, or bad. He even starts out by warning them to watch out for those who "talk the talk," but don't "walk the walk."

He tells us that we will be able to recognize good people by the way they talk and by the way they act.

Those who are truly good will produce good things, and you will be able to see this by the good things that they do.

The longer that we walk this walk with the Lord, the more "fruits of the Spirit" we should be producing.

There should be tangible evidence of change coming out of us!

How many times have you noticed people around you who talk a good talk but don't produce good things in the way that they act or live?

Can you pinpoint some of the good fruit of the Spirit that you produce in your own life?

Prayer for Day 28:

Father, help me today to begin to reproduce more of the fruits of Your Holy Spirit in my life. Help me to walk in love and joy and peace at all times. Bless me today with the gifts of patience, kindness and goodness! Let gentleness and self-control lead me throughout each day. Help me today Father to become a good fruit bearer for Your Kingdom! In Jesus' Name, Amen.

Scripture Reading for Day 28:

Genesis 1:11-13
Matthew 7:15-20
Galatians 5:22-23

Day 28 Life Challenge Question:

How do you think other people see you?

What is inside of you that will produce good fruit? (The fruit of the Spirit must be inside of us!)

What is your strongest or healthiest fruit?

How is that fruit reproducing in your life?

The fruit of the Spirit evident in your life is Kingdom fruit and should be reproduced daily!

Day 29

Question: Why are you so afraid?

Mark 4:39-40 "He got up, rebuked the wind and said to the waves, Quiet! Be still! Then the wind died down and it was completely calm. He said to His disciples, why are you so afraid? Do you still have no faith?"

Even when we walk in the midst of God's blessings and goodness, we can still grow fearful. Think about Jesus' disciples. They lived with Jesus and went everywhere with Him for three years. They saw and experienced miracles with their own eyes. They saw the water turned into wine, they saw people being healed of their diseases, they saw coins appearing in the mouth of a fish, they saw bread multiplying and dividing to feed thousands.

But as soon a storm appeared in their life, they gave in to the old patterns of fear!

In this scripture, it almost sounds like Jesus is a little "put-out" with His disciples when He looks at them and sees their fear. He says, "why are you so afraid?" It is like He is wondering why they haven't been able to see that Jesus was taking care of them and helping them every day. Maybe He was wondering how they could so quickly forget all the miracles that they had witnessed.

We are no different than the disciples of Jesus' day. We feel good and walk strongly when things are going good, but once a problem starts to rise up, we too cower in fear!

As a child of God, His Spirit lives within us. And if His Spirit is within us, we are stronger than we know. Do you know that His Spirit within you gives you strength to overcome difficulties?

2 Timothy 1:7 says, *"For the Spirit God gave us does not make us timid, but gives us power, love and self-discipline."*

Fear is something we all experience, and fear starts with a thought. What if? What about? What else? When thoughts of fear start to take hold of us, remember whose we are and who is fighting for us. Self-discipline during fear is the ability to handle our fearful thoughts and not let them mislead us.

2 Corinthians 10:5 tells us, *"We demolish arguments and every pretension that sets itself up against the knowledge of God, and we take captive every* ***thought*** *to make it obedient to Christ."*

Our thoughts can detour us, damage us and derail us. Taking our thoughts captive means to take the lies and the fear and replace them with the truth of what God says.

His Word about us is more powerful than any lie the enemy can throw at us!

Jesus wants us to always remember that He is with us, no matter what is going on. Romans 8:28 says, *"and we know that in all things God works for the good of those who love Him, who have been called according to His purpose."*

Hebrews 13:5 also tells us: "Keep your lives free from the love of money and be content with what you have, because God has said, **never will I leave you; never will I forsake you."**

No matter what we are going through now, or will go through in the future, remember what God's Word says! This is the truth that will set you free.

Let everything we go through become a new learning experience. Ask God, what are You trying to teach me through this situation?

How does fear show up in your life?

____

____

____

____

What can you do to overcome thoughts or feelings of fear when they come at you?

Can you write down some of the things that God's Word says about you? (Refer back to Day 3 if you need help remembering.)

Prayer for Day 29:

Father, today I refuse to give in to fear. Help me remember who I am in You. Give me strength to overcome anything that rises up against me, remind me that I am more than a conqueror, through Christ Jesus, just like Your Word says! Help me to bind up and catch hold of any fearful thoughts and to replace them with the truth of Your Word! I declare that I am strong and I am able to overcome! In Jesus' Name, Amen

Scripture Reading for Day 29:

Mark 4:35-41
Romans 8:26-30
2 Corinthians 10:5

Day 29 Life Challenge Questions:

What old patterns or old ways have you gone back to during a recent storm in your life?

What can you do to conquer fear in your life when storms arise?

Name a lesson you have learned from a recent storm you've been through.

Day 30

Question: How salty are you?

Matthew 5:13 "You are the salt of the earth. But if the salt loses its saltiness, how can it be made salty again? It is no longer good for anything, except to be thrown out and trampled underfoot."

Be Salt

Salt is good. Salt is a preservative. Salt is a flavor enhancer. Sprinkle some salt on your food and the flavor changes. Salt that has no taste is useless.

Cover your food with salt and it will become inedible. A little salt goes a long way, yet Jesus tells us that we are the salt of the earth. We are to take His message of truth to the world, and sprinkle it everywhere we go, like salt. We are not told to pour it on top of people to the point where they become hardened and angry and are turned off by what we are saying.

Everywhere we go, we take the Holy Spirit with us. Our words and our actions should be like sprinkling salt and leaving a nice taste behind. The atmosphere around us should be enhanced by the love of Jesus working in and through us. Don't lose your saltiness.

Leave the flavor of the Lord everywhere you go.

Be Light

Matthew 5:15 says, *"Neither do people light a lamp and put it under a bowl. Instead, they put it on its stand and it gives light to everyone in the house."*

Light was not created to be hidden. Light brings forth life to everything it touches. Nothing can live very long without light.

John 8:12 tells us that Jesus is the light of the world. It says: *"When Jesus spoke again to the people, He said, I am the light of the world. Whoever follows me will never walk in darkness, but will have the light of life."*

We, as followers of Jesus, are filled with His light! Wherever we go, the light and love of Jesus should shine all around us. People should look at us and think, "there is just something different about them."

Light penetrates darkness! We are to live our lives to bring glory and honor and light into the brokenness of the world around us. We are to live out Matthew 5:16 in our lives: *"In the same way, let your light shine before others, that they may see your good deeds and glorify your Father in Heaven."*

Fill the space around you with His light.

Be Yeast

Yeast is a naturally occurring element that multiplies rapidly by dividing and expanding.

In Matthew 13:33 Jesus taught us that, *"...the Kingdom of Heaven is like yeast that a woman took and mixed into about sixty pounds of flour until worked its way all through the dough."*

You can take a bowl of dry flour and set it on your kitchen counter and it will still be dry flour years down the road. It will not change. But, if you add water and yeast to that flour and mix it up, it immediately begins to change. The mixture starts expanding and growing! It only takes a small amount of yeast to cause a whole lot of flour to rise!

We are to be l like yeast. The world around us is as dry as flour and we are to fill it with the "water of the Word" (Ephesians 5:26) and the love of the Lord. True love and true light is just like yeast, it can't help but multiply!

Spread love like yeast.

Be salt – sprinkle it everywhere.

Be light – go shine in the darkness.

Be yeast – multiply and spread the message of the Kingdom.

List some ways that you can move forward and become salt, light and yeast to the world around you.

____

____

____

____

____

Prayer for Day 30:

Father, I see the world around me and I know that it is in desperate need of Your truth and Your love. Help me to walk into every situation and every circumstance and bring Your light, Your truth and Your love. Shine through me today and every day. I pray that my life will always flavor the world around me with Your love and Your goodness. In Jesus' Name, Amen.

Scripture Reading for Day 30:

Mark 9:50
Matthew 5:13-14
Matthew 13:33

Day 30 Life Challenge Questions:

Have you begun to know who you are in Christ, and what your purpose is in this life?

What have you learned about yourself and what God thinks of you through this thirty day study?

You are loved! You are wanted! You are needed! If you aren't convinced of this, go back and do the thirty days again until you believe who you!

"Run away from childish indulgence. Run after mature righteousness—faith, love, peace—joining those who are in honest and serious prayer before God. Refuse to get involved in inane discussions; they always end up in fights. God's servants must not be argumentative, but a gentle listener and a teacher who keeps cool, working firmly but patiently with those who refuse to obey. You never know how or when God might sober them up with a change of heart and a turning to the truth, enabling them to escape the devil's trap, where they are caught and held captive, forced to run his errands."

2 Timothy 2:22-26 (The Message Translation)